THE FIRST MEN'S GUIDE TO CLEANING HOUSE

•••••••••••••••••

Forthcoming by E. Todd Williams

The First Men's Guide to Baking

How to Manipulate Flour and Sweeteners to Achieve Immoral Power Over the Lives of Other Human Beings

The First Men's Guide to Care for the Elderly

How to Abandon Your Aged Parents and Not Wind Up on the Front Page of Your Local Newspaper

The First Men's Guide to Children's Birthday Parties

How to Arrange It So That Your Child's Worst Enemy Is Savagely Attacked By a Performing Chimp

Interested in seeing these titles in print? Call St. Martin's at your earliest convenience and threaten the life of my editor, Jim Fitzgerald. Please be careful to mention the need to upgrade my royalty arrangements.

THE FIRST MEN'S GUIDE TO CLEANING HOUSE

How to Do a Job That's Bigger Than
You Are On the Strength of Your
Admittedly Puny Endowments

Cheerfully Incomplete in One Volume

E. TODD WILLIAMS

St. Martin's Press ~ New York

FOR VEL-VEL AND ETL,

WHO KNEW NOT WHAT THEY WROUGHT

The First Men's Guide to
Cleaning House

Copyright © 1993 by E. Todd Williams

St. Martin's Press
175 Fifth Avenue
New York, N.Y. 10010

Designed by E. Todd Williams

Library of Congress Cataloging-in-Publication Data

Williams. E. Todd
The first men's guide to cleaning house: how to do a job
that's bigger than you are on the strength of your admittedly
puny endowments / E. Todd Williams.
              p.   cm.
          ISBN 0-312-09021-8
1. Men...Life skills guides...Humor
2. House cleaning...Humor
              I. Title
      PN6231.L33W49   1993
  818'.5402... dc20   92-43885
              CIP

First Edition: March 1993

10 9 8 7 6 5 4 3 2 1

Thanks, Kathy.

TABLE OF CONTENTS

ACKNOWLEDGMENTS

The book you hold is all things to all people.

It has been embraced by both major political parties and serves as the constitution of the state of Virginia.

It was the prototype of the Camp David Accords and the only volume the Dalai Lama carried with him to freedom on his flight from Lhasa Apso. He kept it with him as far as Tinga Layo, but lost it in the salsa at Taco Bueno.

World leaders describe it as a source of consolation. De Klerk and Mandala read it jointly; it shared pyre space with Indira Gandhi. It was clutched to the breast of Margaret Thatcher when she was strapped to an Exocet heading toward the Falkland Islands—the only thing, sadly, that survived the impact.

Foreign readers should take careful note that this is a special treasure of the American people. It's a talisman for deconstructionists, a taliswoman to ethnic feminists, and a big plate of doughnuts for my cousin Bob.

The late Robert Frost, famous vicious poet, called it "the road I wish I had taken." Madonna herself has labeled it "seminal."

For all of this, I am humbly grateful. No—thank *you*, America, for making me strong.

INTRODUCTION

Way back when, when we were a great world power, American men knew how to clean house. They sat around in chairs, scratching crevices, and made vaguely threatening remarks to their wives. Since domestic violence hadn't been invented as a concept, none of the womenfolk took offense. In fact, most of them felt that a jerk in a chair was a whole lot safer than the mobile version.

And best of all, they did the work. Not because it was fun or interesting. How much fun can a phlegm wad be? But because that's the way it had always been: women holding hands with Hoovers. Why would anyone mess with the will of God?

Those days, of course, will come again. Five years tops, ten thousand maximum. I can see the day we'll come home from work to see the little woman, coiffed and powdered, reaming toilets with a thirty-foot plumber's snake.

Until that time, things could get worse. In fact they're getting worse already. Just today the *Wall Street*

Journal said that Matsushita had bought Wyoming and a handsome toolshed belonging to Leona Helmsley. It seems they needed site security for a very important piece of sushi. Next time around they could buy you.

For now, however, you're on your own. Your wife checked out of life-long housekeeping about the time that IBM made you a featured victim of corporate downsizing. So kiss that full-time maid good-bye; she's too busy doing neurosurgery. That was then and this is now: Dirty sinks are your affair.

fig. 1. Woman laughs at one man imprisoned in a force field, while another impales himself on his own umbrella. Relations between the sexes are a constant challenge.

My best advice is to think brave thoughts. Think "America." Think "frontier." Think about a national policy of imposing crippling tariffs on every import.

And mostly think about those three used grapes that have somehow lodged in the crease of the sofa and how exactly you're going to get them out. Ready or not, life *intensifies.* Just like goat cheese in the drawer of the refrigerator. Bottom left, under the penicillin.

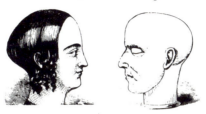

fig. 2. There are fundamental differences between men and women. When their heads are cut off, women keep their eyes *open.*

The trouble with housecleaning is that it takes real skill. And that, my friend, is where I come in. You may be the very King of Implants, but where I come from that's weezing juice. A real man knows when to scrub and when to say he's done his best. The key, as always, is reasonable expectations and the certain knowledge that, if you ignore it, there's at least a chance it will go away.

So listen, pilgrim, and listen good; I'm only going to say this once. There is a future for a man of peace, but he sure as hell better do good window.

CHAPTER ONE

IN THE REALM OF THE SENSELESS

If this were half the book it should be, I'd have all the advice you'd really need. Little things, like disinfecting bathtubs or cleaning jail cell food slots for deposed hotel queens. Or "How to Get Your Garage Floor Sparkling for a Small Soirée with Nancy and Little Brain."

I'd be Heloise herself, telling you how to vaporize those pesky fur balls, or about massaging rodent leavings out of your grandmother's tatwork. I'd be Mr. Clean from Hell, bare of chest and disapproving, with hints on handling nuclear waste. My God what that man did for earrings and harem pants. Talk about cultivating a personal style. Talk about dressing like you really *meant* it.

It'd all be fun in a kind of ruin-your-Saturday way. There are some people who like to have their Saturdays ruined. That bearded careerist who ran "This Old House" has positively made a life out of ruining people's Saturdays.

His basic idea is that you wake at dawn, pack your piece with wire staples, and pump away until you dissolve your elbow. Then you solder tubing until the cows come home, top it off with a tapenade of spackling compound, and broil threepenny nails for dinner.

fig 3. Children beg their mother's permission to touch a giant fur ball on a household pedestal. Involving children in housecleaning may be fun for everyone.

I shouldn't cast aspersions on the lives of television gurus, particularly since I'd like to be one. But that just isn't my idea of Saturday morning. Think hard before you enter that alternative universe. If you do, don't forget that it's a *big* old universe. That guy is part of it, but you've got better things to do than recaulk all the windows in suburban Pittsburgh.

My best advice is to leave the hard stuff for the experts, or forget it entirely because it will make you sick and die. First off, none of this is in the purview of this book. For $9.95, you get an amusing tome. That's author talk for "Laugh, or I'll kill myself." It's about a few simple things you can do at home; none is likely to take longer than a commercial.

Women will buy it because they are angry with men. Men will buy it as an appeasing token. You can hold it front of your enraged spouse or girlfriend and whine that you are at least *trying* to get your life together. The deal is that, for $9.95, the best you get is an appeasing token. Remember that life is an unmerited gift. It is not a meditation on stained upholstery.

Second, I'm not sure that *I'm* up to the hard stuff. I know that's unsettling; I'm supposed to be the expert. The truth is that I'm quarrelsome and depleted. All my friends have chronic fatigue syndrome and wish me ill for my occasional productivity. Don't look to me for Mr. Wizardry. Let someone else tell you the secret recipe for Windex that you can make for pennies *in your very own home!* I could be an expert, but I'm just a guy like you, recovering from twelve years of trickle-down presidents.

Finally—and this is the real issue—to do the job right, to get the meanest dirt out of the most release-resistant contexts, you need carbon tetrachloride, an ancient effluent that makes anthrax or dioxin look like juleps on the porch. Witches used it for spree killings during plague years. The Incas *loved* it for shrinking the heads of decapitated adversaries so that they could be used as balls in Losers Die Lacrosse.

fig. 4. Incan musician playing "Wipe Out" on ceremonial drum, while severed heads look on with interest.

Try not to be frightened when I share the news that carbon tetrachloride is the stuff of madness. Smell it; ha! It will melt your nose hairs. The follicles themselves will close and scar. It cannot be held in normal containers. The little jars in which they sell it are manufactured on an outlying moon of Jupiter out of quartz ions, yew bark, and the pure souls of Venusian slave children. Carbon tetrachloride will kill you on sight. Dirt that mean was meant to stay forever.

So give it up, guy, that sad perfectionism. Put aside that monomania and chug a Bud with Barb and Poppy. That old house will do just fine, and I don't give a rat hair about anyone who says otherwise. Especially if it's that TV guy. Would you trust a person who wears a leather apron with phallic fetish objects tucked into every other loop?

There's only one white whale and he already got Ahab. I guess what I'm saying is that the brine thing's been done.

CHAPTER TWO

THIS GOES HERE

Every good housecleaning is an act of fascism. That is probably why the Germans are so good at it.

Don't get me wrong, I like the Germans. I start each day with a plate of blood sausage. How I love it when those babies ooze! Knock 'em back with a Ruhr Valley Soda: orange juice, pilsner, and an acid rain chaser. All of it seems so real, so fresh, like breaking the heads of Turkish guestworkers.

I will admit that this sounds stern, but somebody here has to be strong for all of us. At least that's what they say in Bonn, and the same is true of household objects: If it won't cooperate, stick it with a knife.

And that, in a *pfefferkorn*, is what housecleaning is about. The boring, awful, unalterable fact is that cleaning house is an act of ordering. You need to establish borders and patrol the forests. Every pile of yesterday's newspapers is a potential source of radio magnetism. It will attract bank statements, instruction manuals, and Nixon's presidential papers. Every conceivable kind of junk will wind up in the pile on the dining room table.

The only way to cope with all of this is to be black-leather, soldier-of-fortune ruthless. Take no prisoners and reprimand your loved ones.

fig. 5. Children scramble for their morning blood sausage treat. Note the ornamental potato puffs on the young child at the left.

Mother's Day calls for special vigilance. For reasons long inscrutable to me, my children insist on homemade Mother's Day cards. This is an especial fetish of my semi-adorable four-year-old. Six months minimum before the big day, the director of her preschool purchases a metric ton of doilies. These are *used* doilies so that she can stay within budget. Four days later she takes delivery on glitter. Thirteen boxcars from the Santa Fe Railroad are diverted to the school on a specially constructed spur.

From that point forward my daughter and her classmates embark on a sweatshop effort of frenzied scissors work. Day and night beneath bare fifty-watt bulbs, they cut and paste their way to heaven. Three shifts daily, half-hour breaks, with an occasional snack of rice and limeade.

The result is a gorgeous, sticky mess: a tatty piece of ersatz Victoriana, trailing wrinkled curling ribbon and globbed with Elmer's. My wife professes to love it thoroughly and six hours later I throw it out. Not in any obvious way, but surreptitiously while everybody's eating. I slink upstairs with an empty shopping bag, stuff it quick and haul the trash. Two days later somebody notices and I feign ignorance on the entire subject. I do not like to see children suffer, but a *little* Stalinism never hurt anyone.

Another thing I like is bins. Plastic bins in different colors. This is another reason my wife despises me. Just this morning she strafed my politics and called me a "Larval Republican Chairperson." But at least she never sends me cards.

Back to bins, she seems to think that normal furnishings should be made of wood. She likes natural things, like cloth and leather, and feels that we ought to live in "comfort." All I can think of is taffeta swags and occasional pillows dipped in chintz. With cabbage roses or people from England tonguing parts from disemboweled foxes. Her personal hero is any slightly overweight man who designs fragile upholstery fabrics for money.

fig. 6. A promising motif for Anglostyle upholstery lovers. Hounds tear at the flesh of a boar while the man at the left stabs his mouth. Such whimsy can relax a room that may otherwise be too stiff or fussy.

Me, I like the look of bins. I buy 'em by the carload from my daughter's preschool. Every color, every manufacturer, although I will admit a passing preference for anything by Rubbermaid. This is *not* another cheesy endorsement, and neither are the other endorsements in this book. Suggestive, yes. Cheesy, no. All are the result of careful research, hours of meditation, and substantial payoffs. I love those big ones that look like pet caskets. My favorite color is that smart slate blue.

I myself use them for everything: dogs in one, hamsters in another. The overriding principle is one thing, one place. The minute you start mixing, it's chintz curtains for everyone. You'll end up with something perfectly awful, like salad, say, or multiculturalism.

It's an especially good idea for a house with kids. When you say "Clean up your room" to an eleven-year-old, it registers as a cross between Latin and Magyar: "*Noofram pizzy clapsha, nik-nik possrep.*" This is an actual transcription from my own son's brainpan. You might as well be talking Basque to the King of Spain.

But when you say, "Put all your condoms there," any child will understand immediately. And when "there" is actually a small plastic bin, conveniently bolted to the top of his headboard, there's at least a chance that order will prevail.

The look you want is industrial shop floor: hard-rock maple for horizontal surfaces, with steel grids everywhere as attachment points for storage. It's the look that made America great. For something lighter try twelve-foot I-beams.

None of this is etched in stone. Back at our house, things are tight. It would be only natural to follow the crowd and put our garbage under the sink. That's what they did on "Ozzie and Harriet"; what's good for the Nelsons is good enough for me. Unfortunately, that's no longer possible; Ozzie's already there in a Rubbermaid. I simply couldn't bear to say good-bye.

The thing to do is to keep on top of it. You could even design a little ritual. Come home, eat, call a friend. Got out drinking, catch a movie. Drive downtown and walk around. Think about cleaning the master broom closet. Go to sleep. That's what's wrong with organized religion. None of the rituals are any fun.

fig. 7. "Come home, call, eat a friend."

By the way, some things need drawers. Generally speaking, they're little things that might attract attention in an open bin. I think immediately of stolen subway tokens or anything made from an endangered species.

Other things are simply too ugly. The classic case is the fitted sheet. No intelligence, however great, is strong enough to fold it cleanly. The North Vietnamese once asked Kissinger what to do with folded sheets. All he did was shrug his shoulders. From that gesture came peace with honor.

Back to that stuff I said about Germans, I rush to say that I didn't mean any of it. I'm a modern man, free of prejudice. All I want is a plate of *schnecken* and the cast recording of *The Rape of Poland*. Got a problem? Build a ghetto. It's just a different kind of bin. No sense getting typhus on *everyone*.

fig. 8. German couple embracing warmly while a broom and a stick ponder unification. Note the clever belt caddy for caustic agents.

CHAPTER THREE

CUT THE RUG

Don't even talk about wall-to-wall.

It's a risk I know to be so negative. This is the second chapter that's opened oozing a mild but vaguely rank vituperativeness. I sort of care about you very much, and I want to see you succeed as a housecleaner. More than that, there's a brand-new Lexus that won't get bought unless you buy this book.

It's come to the point where I just can't help it. The derailleurs on my bike are shot to hell. The spruce out front is thick with bag worms. My mother wonders if my fingers work, since I haven't dialed in sixteen months. The kids passed "insubordinate" yesterday and are homing in on "criminally insane."

Worst of all, those dogs called critics keep commenting on the pattern of my so-called "shamelessness." According to them I use my problems to induce the public to buy my books. Take it from me: I suffer plenty. But trading on pain? Not my style. Buy my books because they're irresistible, not because you care about my end-stage leprosy.

Aside from that I'm right about carpeting. The dirtiest thing you'll ever know is the fibrous mat under the living room furniture. Plush cut, industrial, sculptured, whatever; it doesn't matter what was foisted on you. It's got more crannies than a Defense Department budget and more surprises than a Supreme Court confirmation hearing. Somewhere special where you can't see it is something ready to ruin your future.

Just ask NASA. The current theory is that distant dwarf stars are a shot of hydrogen with lime green shag. They take in everything and hold it tight; don't expect to get light from shag. Very large insects also live in carpet, feeding on dust and spores from houseplants. How about that for a waking nightmare: Africanized bees in Baby's bath mat.

fig. 9. Woman smacks carpet flora with a hammer. The device in her left hand is used to electrocute dust mites. Extreme measures like this may still be necessary.

Worse than that, you're dealing with a target. When something slips, it always *falls*. You wouldn't think so, but it's a fact. In an equitable world, where bad things were apportioned, half of everything would slip and rise. You'd be carrying coffee, lose your balance on a chew toy, and suddenly your ceiling would be splattered with brown.

As it stands, it's always the floor. Dogs know it and see it as a gift. Nothing appeals like the rich absorptiveness of a fresh expanse of wall-to-wall. Jute and urine; it's canine heaven. It's a dead-on bull's-eye in the recesses of the cerebellum. Besides the appeal, there's the issue of hydraulics. I'd hate to see the back end of a dog that could leave a puddle on the ceiling of the family room.

You could ask your kids; they know it too. Little Wayne, the child next door, came to visit the day we moved in. The glass of water should have had us worried, but who could resist those pleading eyes? And who could stop him when, then and there, he favored all of us with a golden shower? Never in time has so much urine cascaded from the body of so small a child. Witnesses say it poured from his eyes.

And once it's there, it's there for keeps. Don't be fooled by that twaddle about Scotchgarding or bogus claims about "Stainmaster" protection. The basic fact is that everybody lies. You lie. I lie. Everybody does it. My very own father has been selling carpet for a century. When I asked him for the inside scoop on broadloom he started prattling about stain-resistant finishes. A little persuasion cleared the air. The next time you catch your father in a lie, threaten to expose his unburied carcass. Truth will dawn like the Day of Judgment.

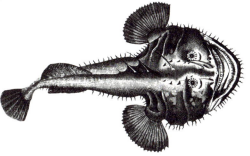

fig. 10. If you look closely at a carpet, you may see a variety of wildlife. This goosefish was spotted in an acrylic plush.

Back to stains, don't be misled. The commercials say you've got nothing to worry about. Little Wayne finishes up in the den and proceeds to dismember a dog in the living room. Two seconds later, Mom's on the scene, thanking God she's got virgin nylon with Stainmaster.

What DuPont conveniently fails to say is that *this particular Mom* is a droid, who has been genetically encoded with chromosomes from a cheetah. If you were a droid, you could do it too. You could get bloody entrails off the Shroud of Turin. The only thing that matters is speed. When that fails, you might as well hang it up.

A real-time stain knows something about loitering. It's got time to brood; it stews and seeps. Very occasionally, it will go productive. Once last year I saw a juice stain profitably employed as an IRS auditor. Most of the time, it sits and sings:

> *Love those fibers, so absorptive!*
> *O that backing feels so good.*
> *What a lovely piece of foam pad.*
> *Let's see just how far I reach.*
> *Here we are, ground floor at last;*
> *They'll never free me from the floorboards.*

Funny thing about stains in carpets: Everything sounds like *The Song of Hiawatha*.

My point is simply that stains are stains because most are more than five minutes old. If Wayne drips long and often and you don't see it, you might as well kiss the rug good-bye.

The alternative, of course, is carpet squares. The theory here is that broadloom's great, but patchwork broadloom's even better. Got a pet who's gone incontinent? Forget that anxious, demeaning watchfulness. Just put the bugger on a carpet checkerboard and lift the squares that can't resist him.

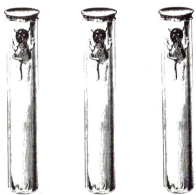

fig. 11. Extreme close-up of carpet stains, expressing pleasure in their own success.

The problem here is size and scale. Carpet squares are a pretty good thing, but only if you happen to live at the Pentagon. They need a base of poured concrete and a staff of thirty to keep them flat. And another thirty to replace the bad ones. And another thirty to make the replacements look six years old just like the others.

By Pentagon standards that's no big deal. There's a staff of thirty to read the paper. There's a staff of thirty to drink the coffee.

fig. 12. Lifting anything, even a carpet square, requires good support in the lower back. The nodules on the interior of this protective belt are actually case-hardened bagels.

But unless you own a failing superpower entirely populated by numskull taxpayers, you're going to have to do without. Leave the squares to the *really* big boys. After all, they kept us safe. If it weren't for them we'd all be dead. Remember what they did to Gorbachov's forehead.

CHAPTER FOUR

A VACUUM OF POWER

So what's a good old boy to do? If you've got a carpet, dump it quick and spend your money on real flooring. If you can't do that, then swallow hard and mosey on out to buy a vacuum cleaner.

First things first: That means no canisters. The little crappers just don't suck. You'd think they would; people buy them. Lots of folks like you and me lay out money and buy a million of them. They're light enough to shlep up steps and they simulate the sound of sucking. Then again, this is a world of newts. At least that's what they say at headquarters. Up at Hoover it's corporate policy. Go ahead and laugh if you want, but those guys put a man in the White House.

A canister vac just can't hack it. The motor's generally much too small and the hose is generally much too long. It might be right for expressing breast milk, but that's another book entirely.

And don't be fooled by hybrid forms. There's an awful mess on the current market with a dinky motor embedded in the canister and a motor wannabe where the hose hits the carpet. I think they call it a "subsidiary motor," but there's at least a chance I'm making that up. What isn't fiction is the gawky pathos of something masquerading as something else. Tell me you don't think "stegosaurus." A thing that needs a little sub-brain to control the movements of its *very own tail* deserves to be made extinct by asteroids.

One alternative is a built-in system. Lots of strong advantages here. The most you'll ever need to lug is a lightweight hose and a few attachments. Get the whisk and the pneumatic carving knife. You might also like the VCR.

The part I like is the raw technology. Smack in the center is Something Big the vacuum guys install in the basement. I've never seen it but I can feel it breathing whenever the house is inordinately quiet. The Very Big Thing is easy to maintain. A few banana chips, fries, and a coke, and it seems to noodle happily for days. For a special treat we order ribs. It's got a thing for the taste of Liquid Smoke.

The rest of the system is just as good. Whenever they bring the thing for the basement, they pass some pipe into the walls of the house. Each length of pipe terminates in a port and when you open the port it revs the engine. What's it like to stuff the port with thirty feet of flexible hose? You'll never know unless you try it, but vacuuming won't be the same again.

The disadvantage here is the freakish cost. A good built-in will cost you plenty, and set you back at least a year. That's the way it is with contractors. They'll need six weeks at least to blast the port holes and then file the report with the EPA. Following that, an OSHA site check and protective clothing for you and the kids. That's to keep the little guys safe from sucking lead with their Cap'n Crunch.

fig. 13. Tending the beast. A built-in vacuum cleaner is a simple machine, but it does take regular attention from its owner. Many built-ins like the taste of chicken, but this one seems to prefer large round lumps.

Of course you may be the kind of father who values lead-based neurological impairment. In that case, skip the protective jump suits. And think again about that tuition savings plan: Vocational school in a Rust Belt enterprise zone is unlikely to cost very much at all.

fig. 14. Construction work calls for protective clothing, but try your best not to skimp on style. A ruff and pom-poms may be just the thing.

What all this means in practical terms is a vote for good old American uprights. You probably knew that all along. The motor's there, right where you need it. It's strong enough to get the big pieces and it's got a brush to do the scut work.

That's the heart of upright vacuuming: The motor runs a rubber belt that makes a little brush revolve. The brush itself is nothing more than a way of striking fear in lint. The lint goes down, it's struck by brushes, and imagines that the end has come. Lying flat in stupefied wonderment, it is now no match for plain old suction. Without the fear, there would be no system. Think of vacuuming as a trip to Haiti. Each little bristle is a Tonton Macoute. It's all a matter of means to ends.

My own machine is an old Eureka, with a motor housing of vintage plastic. What I like is that it's plain and heavy; push it forward and it knows its business, a machine with will and a sense of purpose. It's nicked and dented; the thing has *lived*. The bumper guard is barely there, a weary veteran of savage thrusts for zwieback crumbs that time forgot.

Best of all, it's Shaker plain: no lights, no microchips, no extra anything. It must have come with a box of stuff, but all of it has been scoured away. There's nothing left to fluff the curtains, no special combo of hose and wand to clean between the folds of the radiator.

All of that was desperation: a good idea, a pure clean thought, taffy-pulled to the point of idiocy. You cannot take an upright vacuum and turn it into a Lamborghini. You cannot take a fast-foods franchise manager and turn him into a Republican vice-president. It simply wasn't meant to be. What you want is the Machine Itself, ideally suited to the single task of sucking lint off a level surface.

And note that part about level surface. A fifties ranch house is made for vacuuming. It's a prairie homestead, wide and flat. Nobody likes to plow a mountainside: The American way is horizontal.

fig. 15. An upright vacuum cleaner should be a simple tool. Machines shaped like swans or other avians are likely to lead to tense frustration.

The problem is that at least a few of us live in homes with vertical elements. What that means is steps and landings, the here-to-there of a house with stories. If the steps are wood or covered with tile, refer to the chapter on hard-surface floors. I'd love to tell you all about it here, but nobody paid me to do *anything* twice.

Carpet, though, is another story. If the muscle wall in your lower abdomen can contain the strain of bulging vitals, feel free to shlep your upright upward.

It will work on steps; no doubt about it. In fact it'll probably do just fine. Just think of it as an expedition. My favorite thing is to pull Luciano Pavarotti up the side of Annapurna in February. I like to do it in the middle of the night with defective crampons and rebellious Sherpas.

If that's not your idea of a very good time, you're going to need another tool. My best advice is the Royal Prince. Not that one, silly: He lives in England in a very big house and has lots of money. He paints by number and rants about architecture while England suppurates with racial tension. Read on for the part where he walks the moors, wearing skirts from his estranged wife's wardrobe and imagining the day his mommy dies.

The Prince I mean is a compact "hand-held." It's a long-cord beast with a head of metal, widely merchandised in the yuppie catalogues. Just this once you can believe the hype. The folks at Royal know us guys. The folks at Royal know what makes men strong. Put a Royal Prince in your hand and nobody will mistake you for a woman, ever.

My own machine is a thing of beauty, strong and sturdy with cord to spare. It never knew a crevice it didn't like. It's the perfect complement to those cordless Dustbusters and comes in a plastic version, too. Both of them—the Prince and the Dirt Devil— eat through dirt like pigs gone truffling.

What makes me most especially happy is that little matter of being tethered. I like a hand-held that runs on juice that flows continually from the Grand Coulee Dam. Turn it on and it says *power*. It may just run until the end of time. And God of mercy, it's got a brush that revolves just like big boys do.

Best of all, it holds the dirt in a rubberized bag behind the motor. Turn it on and the bag inflates, a little sausage of dirt-sucking efficiency. Turn it off and it's ready to empty, with no paper liner to gum things up. I love its size, I love everything about it. Got a carpet? Rip it up. Barring that, use a Royal Prince.

The rest of the story is simple stuff. On the level surfaces, use the upright just the way your mommy told you. Big, broad sweeps across the broadloom. Rhythm, amplitude, clean assurance: That's the heart of Iron Man vacuuming. You want the feel of a genuine Serb, searching the village of a despised minority. Push and probe into every corner. Move the furniture; lift the drapery. Who knows where they've hid the samovar?

On the steps it's short, quick strokes. The Royal Prince will let you do it right. It's light enough to handle risers and it won't let you down on simple clean-ups. That's the beauty of a solid hand-held. The other guys may rattle roaches, but who you gonna get to bust the dust?

fig. 16. Trotskyite salesman menaces helpless Tupperware partygoers with a vacuum cleaner bag full of dirt. This could never happen with a Royal Prince.

I also like those little sweepers, the ones that waitpersons use in restaurants. Come to think of it, you might get one, too; just tell the salesperson that you're a manperson. They're not half bad for touch-up work, especially if you've got a nine-year-old who sees the floor as his personal trough.

fig. 17. Corded appliances are both safe and reliable. These interesting items were used in nineteenth-century frontier towns to cast pitying looks on the poor and downtrodden.

But my main squeeze is still the Royal Prince. It's a well-made tool with a nice clean touch. Hold it up and it'll feel just right. It does the work without complaint and seems to understand my needs. In fact, we've managed to become good friends. I want a tool that knows from intimacy. I want a tool that knows my soul.

I'll let you know how it all turns out. He's coming home Thanksgiving to meet my sister.

CHAPTER FIVE

TWO HUSBANDS FOR DONNA'S FLOOR

You'd think I'd be a fiend for no-wax. It's a suburban thing: easy maintenance. And the same is true for installation. There's no fitting tiles or tacky grout work, just a roll of yard goods twelve feet wide. You call the flooring people after breakfast and five minutes later the job is done. It's man-type thing, clean and outward. No dimpled recesses or convolutions.

The stuff is also pretty good, an early product of atomic testing. That Fermi guy would go off to work and come home for lunch trailing globs of "plute." The birth defects were bad enough; the Fermi kids had hairy eyeballs. But the real problem was household maintenance: It made a hell of the Fermi kitchen.

Fermi himself was at a loss, but Mrs. Fermi knew her protons. She marched into her husband's lab and boiled a batch of ionized Crisco. Two small shots of heavy water brought the whole damn thing to term. The resulting brew was an odd elastic that could be poured out flat and allowed to harden.

At this point Mrs. F. was made. She toured the country in the middle of the war, stumping hard for her "no-plutonium floor." When the country failed to grasp her message, she sold the rights for a slow, sweet song. The song she got was "Balm in Gilead." It's the official anthem of the Chernobyl Bugle Corps. Thus the no-wax floor was born.

fig. 18. A look at the Fermi Lab in Los Alamos. Mrs. Fermi is at the right, adding subatomic particles to common vegetable shortening.

My own discomfort is from God knows where. See Chapter 3 for my thoughts on broadloom: When things are large and undifferentiated, an accident has ramifications beyond itself. If you drop the microwave on asphalt tiles, you can remove the pieces that are marred or broken. If you do the same on no-wax sheet goods, you're doomed to replace the whole expanse. Either that or a cob-job patchwork that makes it look like a reassembled chicken.

Beyond that quibble, go for the no-wax. It does the job and it's a cinch to clean. Every product would love to help, but many commit the cardinal sin of too many promises in too small a space. Something should either clean or shine. A concoction that claims to accomplish both—those acrylic hybrids come to mind—offends my sense of spare efficiency. What's it really doing, anyway? If it's busy cleaning, can it produce a shine? And if it's busy shining, how can it clean? And what's the point of a no-wax, anyway, if it needs refreshing with an acrylic cocktail? Somebody here needs sodium pentothal, quick.

What you really need is a sudsy slush that's strong enough to do the job, but gentle on the bio-chemical something that enables the floor to hold its shine. Avoid anything at all that comes in boxes. The little granules will drop from sight, but they'll remain behind to abrade the shine. You've got a friend in Murphy's Oil Soap, although it, too, needs to be mixed with water. The same is true of plain ammonia or Lysol, regular scent or lemon. Later on, I'll rant about mixing, but, in fact, you can't get around it here. Any cleanser made for floors is likely to need to be diluted.

fig. 19. When mixing cleaning solutions, stick to the commonplace. Human body parts are undesirable and may interfere with ease of application.

What you want to avoid is the hell of rinsing. Be careful here of that siren, Pine-Sol. I love the smell and I love its power. But power's always a two-edged sword. Whatever's in it melts through steel: The things it touches can turn to oatmeal. That makes it wrong for wooden floors and moderate trouble for vinyl tiles. You could try it out on no-wax floors, but the label specifically urges rinsing. If you have to rinse, that's it for me. It's bad enough I have to mop up once.

Beyond no-wax is a twilight world of various versions of floor-care purgatory. Floors like these fall into categories. In the first are floors that are The Thing Itself. That means a floor of wood or vinyl or linoleum that presents to the world without a barrier. There's nothing at all between you and it except a coat of old-fashioned floor wax.

A floor like this needs normal cleaning, but it's complicated by the nature of the waxy coating. If the floor is only mildly soiled, treat it just like a soiled no-wax, using the mildest solution of whatever you mix. That will remove the dirt but leave the wax intact, or at least enough of it to come up shining.

If the floor is more than moderately soiled (or there are too many coats of accumulated wax) you'll have to rip the thing to pieces. Here's your chance to go full strength. Use all the things you've used before, but straight from the bottle or in stronger concentrations.

For everything except a wooden floor, Pine-Sol may be your very best bet. It will work its magic on nearly everything and pull right through to the original surface. You could even risk it on asphalt or rubber. Just make sure to rinse it thoroughly. I know I whined about rinsing floors, but removing wax is another story. This is work of a different magnitude and you can't expect to do the job with spit.

For wood, you'll need a different product. Try Murphy's if you've got it handy or a special product made for stripping. The one I've got is Trewax Wood Cleaner. The advantage here is that it will not fail you, although it may very well kill you first. It's now available by prescription only and you have to buy it from the Surgeon General. Me, I'll stick with Murphy's Oil Soap. Up against the likes of Trewax , it's nothing more than refried plasma. But at least I'll live to walk the floors.

When the floors are stripped, you'll need to wax again. God almighty it won't be fun. Unless you like to chew on foil or suck the rumps of African wildebeests, waxing floors will *not* be fun.

The best approach is something in a paste, though it means you'll work on your hands and knees. There are machines to help you out, but each one weighs ten thousand pounds and was last used to clean up vomit from fourteenth-century peasant plague victims. When the recipe calls for heavy metal, get an expert and a nice motel room.

The other category is The Thing Itself Smothered Over with an Acrylic Coating. The classic case is a sealed wood floor, dipped in plastic like a room-sized Dove Bar. Floors like this look cheap to me: a little too shiny for my patrician taste. Poppy would take one look and barf. Me, I'd always go with semigloss.

fig. 20. If you wish to use Trewax Wood Cleaner, you will inevitably need to apply in person. Look for a somber, bearded man sitting alone at a long wooden counter.

These floors want the no-wax treatment: a nice light rinse with nothing special, the very same stuff I recommended above. Try Murphy's, Lysol, or plain ammonia. If that won't do it, nothing will. The stores are full of other products made especially for acrylic coatings. Unless you like to be taken in, my best advice is to breeze on by.

But do not ever neglect a floor. A nice, plain floor is a thing of joy. Wood and tile adore those dust mops that look like English sheepdog road kill. Just remember to spray the mop head so that it clings like love to dirt and dust balls. Easier still is a good attachment that will let you vacuum a hard-surface floor. That way, see, the dust gets sucked instead of moved from here to there. A built-in vac knows how to do this.

fig. 21. A failure to sweep regularly may result in elaborate hair balls. An example like this may take a specialist to remove.

Either way, just try your best. What doesn't kill us makes us miserable, but there's only so much a guy can do. In her heart of hearts, your wife knows this. But even if you fail her big time, there's still some consolation knowing the thing that binds all men together: She'll kill her second husband, too.

CHAPTER SIX

GLASSNOTES

Take my word for it: It was bound to happen. The silly scones never had a chance.

Oh, I know all about the wedding of the century, the virgin princess, the blue-blood background. But the guy was forty by the time they *burped* him. Spiritually dead would be putting it tactfully. Then there's the little matter of The Abnormality. You'd think a man who was the Prince of Wales would at least *occasionally* trim his ears.

Frankly, dears, my heart goes out to her. All those gloomy walks with Charles at Balmoral; the rumored sexual games with Camilla; kissing *old* people right on the mouth. A princess ought to be just folks, but they didn't put *any* of this in the video guidebook.

From that point forward it was Tailspin City: the "calls for help," The Penknife Incident, and that pathetic hour on the steps at Sandringham when she accidently on purpose tried to abort little Will. The last I heard she was roaming Buckingham, fighting off madness with a spray bottle of Windex. As of June, she had done the first floor and was staring vacantly at the Queen Mother's Breakfast Nook. Don't these people know about therapy?

fig. 22. Their Royal Highnesses were mismatched from the start. Here Diana learns that her belly has been sown with a princeling embryo from the demon Charles.

I myself wanted to know more about the windows: Was that regular Windex or a European blend? How many windows in a Joe Average Palace? Are they large enough to squeegee or did she have to use paper towels? And what does she prefer: a foam or a spray? I know that royals watchers had other concerns, but I don't think it's wrong to expect a crumb about housecleaning. I'd also like to know about Princess Michael of Kent. Has it occurred to anyone that she has a man's name? Do they call her son "A Duke Named Sue?"

Speaking about windows, the best thing ever was a breezy feature in *Consumer Reports*. "Breezy" might actually be overstating it: Nothing about *Consumer Reports* is ever breezy. Not with the lab coats. Not with the mattress-testing machines. And not, especially, with the acid-resistant lab stations.

fig. 23. Charles modeling a number of Diana's skirts. The object he holds in the third image from the left is a kneeling effigy of Camilla Parker-Bowles.

I've tried to stay calm about *Consumer Reports*, but all I manage to feel is mounting dread. It invariably sends me into a tizzy of self-loathing: substandard replacement line for my weed eater *again*? Who can remember sixty attributes of evaluation? And who cares whether my choice has a lemony grace note, but impressed two of the panelists as "somewhat rancid and viscous"?

But the article on windows was *Reports* at its best. What's the right thing to use on dirty glass? Practically anything, including *plain old tap water*. But make sure that if it gets more elaborate than that, it's something compounded with ammonia, not vinegar. You want the stuff in the big blue bottles. Leave the green for peasants in the Ukraine.

Believe me when I say that I could have told you that myself. It's a simple matter of anecdotal observations. Vinegar for salads, ammonia for cleaning. Who ever heard of red-wine ammonia? Would you douse your arugula with a tarragon ammonia-ette?

So why did I need *Reports* to tell me? Like most Americans I am prostrate before it. In the world of reporting, only two things are inerrant: Geraldo on satanism and *Reports* on ammonia.

CHAPTER SEVEN

ONE IN A MULLION

But what, pray tell, should you use to wipe with? Some things are too entirely personal, but as long as we stay in the public domain, I'll try to make it worth your while.

Ask a million people what's best for windows and they'll tell you to wipe with yesterday's newspaper. What could be more post-industrially appealing than to put your refuse to a doubled use?

It's a dream come true: the glass-cleaning equivalent of a disposable diaper that could be recycled into paper and then bound with wheat paste into acid-free books. All of which would be about Dr. Albert Schweitzer and his obsessive deference toward hordes of army ants.

The problem is that it's a ruse and a scam, some Greenpeace fantasy like rubber harpoons. If you speak gently to a tuna and treat it right, it will simply dress *itself* in a six-ounce can.

The truth about newspaper is that it's nonabsorbent. If it sucked up liquids it would suck up ink and your editorial page would look like a piece of used Bounty. Marge would take to the waves again, screeching this time about the *Miami Herald*. Try it at home and you'll see what I mean. Your local newspaper may seem like a rag, but all it will do to a spill is relocate it. The only possible exception is the *Manchester Guardian*. All rags, clearly, are not created equal.

fig. 24. The only thing worse than ink-saturated newsprint is a man-sized grasshopper with a taste for nape hair. Try very hard to keep your distance.

Beyond that there's the problem of the ink itself. A window is usually set in a frame and the frame is usually set in a wall. Unless your paper has absolutely nothing to say, the sections you use will be covered with ink. When the paper is wet, the ink will bleed, probably onto any white surface nearby.

The same thing happens when you read the news on the subway. Sixty-three people hyperventilating in fear as your car races through the steaming bowels of New York City generate the same level of wetness as the Gulf of Tonkin.

That's why I personally would never deliver a baby on newspaper, despite the classic, picturesque advice to the contrary. Who wants a kid imprinted with a weather map, or Evans and Novak steamed onto his butt?

There are worse things you can do to a very young child, but all of them involve neoconservative columnists and none could be cleared by my publisher's legal staff. Picturesque advice is generally entertaining but unsuited to the realities of life in this century. Ask anyone who's tried to make a citizen's arrest.

Especially vulnerable are the window's mullions. That's what they say at *Consumer Reports* and they know more than William Casey. A mullion, for the sake of you ignorant pigs, is part of the wooden matrix that frames each pane in a window. If you get ink on a mullion, they cancel your subscription. If you do it again, they send a posse to your home.

The group will arrive under the banner of the Consumers Union, a paramilitary strike force 200,000 strong. My best advice is don't mess with the Union. Each member gets a specially rigged John Deere riding mower that will chew through your lawn and straight to Beijing. Confronting the Union simply doesn't pay off. When it comes to windows, stick with plain paper towels.

fig. 25. An alternative form of punishment by the Consumers Union. A technician arrives in the middle of the night and sucks out your life-force with a highly technical apparatus.

As for the job itself, you're going to need plenty. Understand from the start that you can't do everything. The modern window is a tetragrammaton of complexity. In the average home it's a four-sided monster, each face more frightening than the Whore of Babylon.

There's the inside-inside, the outside-inside, the inside-outside, and the outside-outside. Literalists should note that I made that all up, purely for the pleasure of hearing of my own voice. It's like a chant or a poem from Vachel Lindsay. Perhaps a Navaho prayer for the soul of Tony Hillerman.

What I mean simply is that you've got *two* windows, the original pane and the add-on storm. And each of those units have two separate faces. All of this comes out of my suburbo-centric mindset; if you live in an apartment in New York City, count yourself fortunate if you have a window at all.

The problem, obviously, is that at any given time, two faces at least will be completely inaccessible. They are the outside-inside and the inside-outside. Between them is the pocket of dead, dry air that protects you from the winds that sweep off Lake Michigan. It also manages to preserve forever the mummified exoskeletons of every bug that ever died. Such is the price we pay for comfort: None of us is more than the tomb attendant for a bizarre anthology of extinguished life-forms.

The other price we pay is fundamental well-being. Together, the parts keep us stewing in pollutants that make Love Canal look like a mountain freshet. Radon, solvent fumes, smoke, asbestos particles: Everything goes in and nothing comes out, an oncological festival of nasty penetrants. That's the net effect of doubled windows that can't be opened except with a tire iron. We live and work in a sick-building society. Even my garage is on daily insulin injections.

fig. 26. You may occasionally find the tiny corpses of insects caught between the panes of an exterior window. If you discover anything more exotic than that, your first call should be to the Milwaukee Police Department.

And yet into that pocket no man should go. It means standing on a ladder on a miserable day with all the wrong tools and all the wrong attitudes for a job that is inherently foul and uncivilized. Think of it as a simple matter of priorities. Life in the nineties is about three-man architectural firms and canceled contracts for mall-based Doggie Palaces. It is not about prying a storm window from its frame.

And assuming you could get the damn thing disengaged, how precisely would you get it to the ground? Try to remember that the child who should be standing there, gazing up lovingly at his hardworking father, is watching *Behind the Green Door* on his bedroom entertainment center, utterly spent from his multitudinous exertions.

Most important, you weren't made for this work. Perhaps I should only speak for myself, but a man who was built to joust with Molière, whose mind has the lambent sparkle of Restoration Comedy, has no business wrestling with a balky storm window. You might even pass on the outsides entirely. It's the ladder thing all over again: too high, too hard, too messy and unstable. Leave the exterior windows to the guys in the Yellow Pages. They'll charge you the gross national product of Bolivia, but there's a chance you'll live until your thirty-seventh birthday.

The inside, though, is another story. Everything's accessible and close to the floor. No vertiginous encounters with the iffiness factor. All you have to do is to confront the fact that there are many more windows than you ever thought, all of them are covered with a combination of dog drool and peanut butter, and you will spend the rest of your life trying to keep them clean.

fig. 27. The dangers of using a ladder to clean windows. An armed pumpkin may threaten you with a shotgun and turn your partner into a pulpy filling.

Now, I'm not dumb. I know what you're thinking: "Maybe I'll be the lucky slob this time. Maybe it's truly possible to say that my kind of guy doesn't 'do' windows."

Forget it, Little Brain. It's me or you and I'd rather scrape the core in a five-alarm meltdown. If you think that anyone is going to do your windows, there might be a place for you in Kuwait City. The way I hear it, the zoo's still hiring. Maybe they'll let you bury the flamingos and the coatimondis. Think of windows as a peak experience. It's the can-do task for the can-do guy

The trick, as always, is to be lean and unencumbered: a roll of towels, a receptacle for the dirties, and a single, trigger-style bottle of glass cleaner. Because I'm a purist, the towels should be white. It will be easier to see what comes off the windows (akin to checking your fingernail after putting it in your ear). Besides, there's the little matter of aesthetics. The people who make towels should be dumped on an ice floe. If it's not a border of mushrooms, it's colonial-style kitchen implements, all printed in sepia or sea-foam green. An endless travesty of design for the home; if it were possible, I'd banish them all to Flatbush.

I should probably be saying something about rags. If I were an evolved personality with a brick in my toilet tank, I'd put aside those paper towels for good. Bring on the old T-shirts, the pillow cases, and the button-downs. The trouble is that most won't absorb a thing. That's because they're all at least 15 percent plastic, and polyester absorbs about as much as cubic zirconium. What's good for a shirt (see *The First Men's Guide to Ironing*, written by me) is not necessarily good for wiping a window.

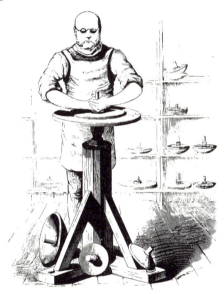

fig. 28. It is possible to make your own paper towels at home, but it is best to leave the cardboard rollers to experts.

The second big problem is the matter of time: If you use rags for windows, you're gonna need to wash them and the purpose of this book is to get the job done *now*. All right, Greenpeace, shoot me in the chest.

I deserve it; I asked for it; I'm entitled to die. But figure it this way: If you're home washing rags, whose gonna save those poor little bottle-nosed dolphins? Who's gonna ram those Japanese trawlers?

As for the bottle of glass cleaner, the choice is yours. I covered the basics in the chapter previous. It was ammonia there and it's ammonia here.

It's possible, of course, to mix your own cleaner, using ammonia, tap water, and nothing else. You'll find the recipe on the back of the ammonia bottle. Then again it's possible to cure your own venison in the guestroom and dig a root cellar for your surplus sweet potatoes. A rice paddy might look nice in the bathtub. My soul rebels against mixing anything.

So which is better: Glass Plus or Windex? I decided to communicate directly with the manufacturers, asking pointed questions about glass-cleaning arcana.

The DowBrands company, makers of Glass Plus, offered early decision for my son at Northwestern and property on the choice northern shore of Nantucket. When I balked about the way Glass Plus stains on acrylic, they thought I might enjoy Gstaad this summer and the corporate getaway in the Guernseys next spring. All in all, a most generous offer.

Windex, on the other hand, seemed to know all about vintage speedboats and took a genuine interest in my first-edition Faulkners. I loved their idea about Princeton's program in European literature and I think the little guy will be happy in his own apartment. Besides, they sent me a Godiva ballotin simply for the pleasure of allowing them to bid.

The way I figure it, it's Windex by a hair.

Chapter Eight

Windows and Orphans

All of which brings us to winning the West.

If there's anything good about cleaning windows, it's that all the best spray bottles come equipped with triggers. I don't know about you, but for me that's a comfort. Makes me think about blood sports and covert operations. Focuses the mind on abandoned children. Manifest Destiny waits for no one.

Back at the picture window, begin with a trigger tug. The resulting spray should be a fine, light mist. If you're living right, you'll have an adjustable nozzle that can be set for tiny droplets and maximum coverage. Think of woodland faeries flecked with dew. After all, they're always thinking of you.

If the window's big, do it in sections, wiping firmly, beginning at the top. You'd think something like this would be obvious to most people, but most people thought the Khmer Rouge were "offensive, but tolerable."

If you do the bottom and then spray the section over it, run-off from on high will spoil your efforts. The same is true if you're painting a wall. I've seen so-called normals begin chest-high without realizing the effects of gravity on paint. It might sound harsh, but people like that should be locked in a very small closet at birth and fed on kibble shoved through a hole.

fig. 29. A freshly cleaned window is a gift from the gods. Here grateful dervishes dance the blues away.

Most people get the trigger bottle right. It's the wiping clean that throws 'em for a loop. It looks like it's working, you get some English in the towel, and what's left at the end is worse than what you started with. It's what *Consumer Reports* calls "streaks" and "smears." Nobody knows what they are or where they come from. But the window looks like it has been cleaned with olive oil or like somebody's applied a booger with a putty knife.

Part of the problem is the vagaries of weather. For confusing reasons having to do with particle physics, the warmer the window, the more easily it wipes. You'd definitely have to go subatomic for an explanation. I keep a set of quarks in a pen in the back yard, but they seem just as confused about the issue as I am.

The other part is pure human laziness. It's the pathetic willingness of cretins like you to settle for orange roughy, frozen in squares in Auckland, New Zealand, in 1971. You're a middle-class guy with every advantage, a slightly sluggish mutual fund, and a reasonable lay-up. And yet you're willing to tolerate less-than windows.

Wake *up*, mister. Get with the program. Be sparing with the spray, use clean paper towels, and wipe the damn window like you really mean it. And if it films or streaks, do it again. There's no substitute here for masculine task focus except paying a bundle to have it done for you. I call that a pretty poor version of machismo. Maybe we should just call it "machismette."

Once you're done, go on to the next pane and keep on going until you're dead and buried. Count your blessings; it will be over when you are. They don't ask you to do windows in the world to come. The only people who do them there are certain members of the

Senate Judiciary Committee. Think of it as a get-even thing. Unfortunately, very few people know about it.

The nice part is that windows keep for a while. Figure bimonthly for a nuclear household. Unless, of course, you have a storm door and your storm door serves a family with children.

In that case you can forget even the hope of happiness: You'll be enslaved to the door and its pattern of sticky fingerprints until they can't find a vein that's worth the trouble.

My best advice is to get an abused hunting dog who becomes enraged at the sight of little children. Station him in the foyer and warn the little ones that bad things will happen if they touch the storm door. Very occasionally, this has an effect, although the child-welfare people may decide to add to your file. As far as I'm concerned, it's a small price to pay.

I wish I could end on a note of encouragement, but I'm afraid that it's just as bad as you think. All my brave talk about energy and exertion is nothing compared to the unalterable fact that a twentieth-century window is impossible to clean.

At the very moment you're done with slaving there will still be three separate surfaces as virginally dirty as the moment you began. However clean the inside may be, it will never look as if you've accomplished anything. I'm sorry about that, I really am. But don't blame it on me; I just write the books. On a clear day, you can't see forever.

fig. 30. If you can't persuade your child to avoid smudging the storm door, it may be necessary to put him back.

You could try to keep things in proper perspective. You were never deposed as a head of state. And if you *happen* to be the late Haile Selassie, at least you aren't married to Raisa Gorbachov.

CHAPTER NINE

A RICH FANTASY LIFE

So what should you think about when you're cleaning the house? One thing for sure, it's not cleaning the house.

I occasionally make a great big deal about the dignity of housework, about the rhythm of accomplishment. I talk about reaching the sponge mop within, about planting a garden of domestic affirmation.

In actual fact, it's a grotesquely large lie, based on my uncanny ability to generate interest in books that promise grinding struggle without visible reward. Clean the kitchen and it will be dirty by dinner. Put Sisyphus in front of a boulder or a dishwasher and he would be hard-pressed to distinguish the slightest difference.

My best advice is to block it out altogether, to establish a psychological elsewhere of imaginary endeavor. I generally begin with the shaft of light that pours from the oculus in the library scene in *Citizen Kane.* You know the shaft: It's the giant dust beam that defines the power of black-and-white cinema.

As soon as I get there, I've got enough to carry me. Hand in the garbage disposal, pulling celery fiber from the blades, I imagine myself a media wunderkind. I'm writing scripts for radio, scaring the pants off the citizenry—a legendary talent in my early twenties.

Urine on the carpets? I don't even notice. I'm up to my earballs in theater for the masses, a proletarian impresario for the new American century. There's talk that I'll be given a studio of my own, a community of artists to embody my vision.

By the time I hit the toilet bowl, I'm the Biggest Knish—young and accomplished and wealthy beyond imagining. Women long for my attention; the populace adores me. I control my product down to the typography on the credits list. Could human life get better than this?

Well, no, not exactly, but it could be worse. It could be *my* life we're talking about here: the grunty story of a bland little guy unfit for happiness, unfit for fortune, unfit for Orson Welles to spit on. A guy who spends his formative years picking his nose in deep right field is not a likely candidate for maturity and confidence.

Like that day in June when the air conditioning went and my support group was due at three for mineral water. I went to my fantasies, but nothing clicked: no shaft, no theater company, no studio, no women. Well, maybe the shaft. But not much else.

All that appeared from the depths of my imagining was a bloated guy wearing a size-eighty turtleneck. He was drinking Ripple and making commercials and everybody said that he had squandered his talent on tawdry projects of dubious merit.

fig. 31. Welles and companion attend Oscar ceremonies in the sixties. Her gown is actually two Bob Mackie originals.

I keep trying to tell you that housecleaning isn't easy. In the worst of times, Orson hired it out. Don't ask me how; I just happen to know. Well, maybe I said it would be somewhat easy. Any which way, I was probably lying.

CHAPTER TEN

DUST THOU'D BETTER

There's nothing manly about dusting furniture. I regret it plenty, but I'm afraid it's true. It brings to mind those blue-haired ladies with their awful little globs from Hummel. Porcelain ponies wreathed with daisies. Tiny woven baskets with fruit. Treacly, bulbous German children, dressed in lederhosen made of clay.

Not even the Germans can stand this stuff. That's why they started World War II. Their real aim wasn't world domination, but to reclaim every figure they ever made. They couldn't help it; Wotan forced them. He said he'd confiscate their poison gas toys.

Yet here and there, men have dusted. Shopkeepers dust; so do curators. That is, in fact, their primary purpose. Ask yourself what you would do if you spent your entire acquisitions budget on an Etruscan jam jar? How about *half* a budget on a Late Bronze fondue set? Worser still, a T'ang orange juice glass? This is the stuff on which reputations are made. My guess is that you'd do the dusting. Minute Maids are plenty good, but some things call for special handling.

Many curators, of course, are men. Presumably, then, real men dust. But it's an open secret that real men don't. I hear whining: "So who's a man?" If you have to ask, just give it up; there's a very good chance that you're a box of chicken parts.

fig. 32. Remember that cleaning house may mean recycling. Here, piles of dust have been gathered up and shaped into attractive little hats.

A real man eats brains and kidneys. He walks to work past storefront churches and labors in a factory with a noontime lunch whistle. The shoes he wears have metal toes. He could beat you up and say bad things and you'd be lucky to get out alive. He speaks in short declarative statements, without complexities like punctuation. *That's* a man. Go ask your mother. She may still remember what men were like before she met your pantywaist father.

You could always try to dust with gusto. Between us, we could call it "gusting." A man I know, a leader in the drum movement, thinks of dusting as a trial of manhood. He runs a tape of Little Ricky and does his chest in rouge and cornmeal. With Babalu to soothe his soul, the house somehow gets clean enough.

I've tried to pin him down on details, but all I get is nowhere fast. I like the part about the primeval bathtub, but what's this stuff about keys and wounds? And why the hell does Robert Bly wear that vest in every picture *ever*? Inquiring minds demand to know. And yet, along with you, I am uninitiated. Yearning, I stand outside the sweat lodge.

Back to dusting, there's just no choice. It's me or you; dust or be dusted. Make no mistake, the dust will come. It comes from everywhere all at once. Some of it comes from falling leaves. A significant share comes from Salt Lake City. The Tabernacle Choir is dust-intensive, especially the section of male impersonators. Most, however, is a natural by-product of the self-destruction of Michael Dukakis. It began in the fall of 1988. At this point there is no end in sight.

So what to do? Don't be fooled. I know I say that all the time, but I feel obliged to protect the infirm. To hear the talk on daytime television, you've got no future without Lemon Pledge. Cleans and polishes. Dusts and waxes. Does the laundry and walks the dog. I swear I heard the lady say that Lemon Pledge would type your thesis.

fig. 33. Dust comes from everywhere. This shot was taken in October of the ill-fated Dukakis campaign.

For decades now we've heard just about everything, and I don't just mean from Lemon Pledge. The dream of everyone who makes this stuff is a single product that will Do It All.

Sorry residue-head, it just ain't so. If this book has a theme at all, it's that you can't believe what you read or hear. There may be one or two exceptions. I for one believe in music. On alternate Tuesdays, I believe in love. I may also be the last American to believe in the findings of the Warren Commission. Beyond that, I don't believe in anything, much less the claims of Lemon Pledge.

What appeals to me is the single product, singly used for a *single purpose*. Take the case of a wooden chair. Way back when, when men were men, wooden chairs were made of wood. Not hardened resin or processed wood food, but the real thing from real trees. And plenty of it, through and through. A chair was made of oak or maple, not pine veneer over mango Slurpees.

The chair itself would be shaped and sanded and then stained to match the prevailing preference. What happened next was also preference: varnish, lacquer, or plain shellac. A little tung oil or boiled linseed. Each technique has had its partisans, based on strengths and disadvantages entirely incomprehensible to those of us who are nonwoodworking normals. What hasn't changed is the finishing touch. The furniture made before our time was almost always kissed with wax.

fig. 34. Avoid the product that claims to do two things at once. This rug beater/cheese slicer is particularly graceless.

A chair like that may well belong to you. If that's the case, then count your blessings: Unlike us, it can be born again. Like any wood, it may come to look like hell. Cupboard doors get stained with body oils. The same for woodwork in a door or a window frame. Kitchen table rims are a perfect target. If your kids are like the ones I live with, the rim and its underside may soon collect a greenish mass of discarded sneezes.

All of this may mean refinishing, but start out simply with a competent wood cleaner. Nostalgia sucker

that I am, my first choice again is Murphy's Oil Soap.
It used to come in little tubs and had the consistency
of a translucent cold cream. Then again, everything
before 1960 had the consistency of translucent cold
cream.

**fig. 35. The furniture in your home may lack the weightiness
of the classics, even though it is produced in traditional
patterns. How many times have you observed this scene?**

For this we are indebted to Mamie Eisenhower.
While Ike cavorted with Kay in Italy, she perfected the
art of embedding meat in Jell-O. Churchill is said especially to have liked Mamie's justly famed Lime Liver
Medley. Ike is said especially to have liked going over
to Kay's for pasta primavera.

Another possibility is Weiman's Furniture Soap.
I mention it here not because I like it, but because it's
part of product etiquette. Since I mentioned Murphy's
Oil Soap, I should properly offer at least one alterna-

tive. You may have noticed that I rarely do this, but I've decided to repent before I die. Normally, I'm a fanatic partisan and part-time vicious twit, to boot. Very occasionally I manage to see that those I mention may materially reward me.

The problem with Weiman's is the identity thing: Is it a cleaner, a polish, or one of those bastard hybrids? The front label says that it "restores natural beauty." Not only that, but it's made with flaxseed oil. That's polish language, Lech, make no mistake. The back, however, is demurely modest. All it does is remove crud and gunk. Safe for use on three-term congressmen. I'll give it credit for political correctness, but I'm still not sure about its personality.

The other problem is where to get it. The only place to find a tin of Weiman's is at a high-end grocer's in a pricey suburb. The kind that sells personalized sourdough, wrapped in lengths of Hermés scarving. That may describe your local supermarket, but we live quite differently in my squalid zip code. Until I see big piles of royalty checks, it will be some time before I lay in a tin of Weiman's.

Back to the issues, be careful with soaping. Use the right dilutions for the bottled stuff, or make life simpler with a well-made spray. In either case use a clean cloth for wiping. The Murphy's people say to test beforehand and that's the conventional wisdom in the field. Who knows if you got the one odd batch accidentally compounded with Agent Orange? It would be an awful shame to find that out on the dreamy curves of your vintage Steinway.

fig. 36. Man checks for boogers on the underside of a table while a friend looks on. Never do this unaccompanied.

But don't be confused by a product that's working. In defense of Weiman's, it clearly states that soaping furniture (or cabinetry or paneling) will leave the surface dull and lusterless. There should be a Nobel Prize for honesty like that. It almost takes my breath away to hear an American company admit a negative. But Weiman's knows what it wants to do, even if it confuses the issue with flaxseed by-products. When you lather wood you want to take things away, not leave more behind to sabotage the finish.

Speaking of which, the choice is yours. As I said above, the old-time favorite is a finish coat of furniture paste wax. Believe it or not, that's my choice too. I know I'm supposed to say the opposite. Cutting corners is my personal creed. Yet part of me is horse-and-buggy. Just last week I stewed a prune and polished it off with a Latin mass. My favorite thing is to sit at home and read "Sinners in the Hands of an Angry God."

Aside from that, there's nothing nicer than the soft, sweet shine of a very good paste wax. It looks old and real, like Jimmy Stewart. It makes me think of preferential treatment for alumni children at unaffordable colleges. It also happens to be profoundly masculine. There may be nothing manly about dusting furniture, but paste wax is another story. American culture loves the man who loves the paint job on his new Mercedes, or at least loves it enough to keep it safe with a biweekly coat of fresh carnauba.

The other path is some kind of furniture oil. I suppose the results will be roughly similar. All the labels on all the oils ooze with promises about "moisturizing" and "revitalizing." I know there's probably something to this: Unlike everything except the Vampire Lestat, wood has a life beyond the grave. It will respond forever to changes in humidity, drawing water and then de-tumescing like some vaguely comical superannuated satyr. A good furniture oil seems to keep things supple.

fig. 37. Neck strain is inevitable when you wipe surfaces above your head. A nicely dressed chiropractic healer may be helpful in such a situation.

My problem with oil is that it goes on wet and it can leave a greasy film if you use too much. It seems to take more careful calibration to use the right amount of oil than it does to use the right amount of wax. In addition to that, it's a toxic nightmare. The most you'd get by swallowing wax is a votive candle in your large intestine. The most you'd get from swallowing oil is grand mal seizures and bleeding ears.

The only significant drawback to wax is that it responds quite poorly to casual abrasion. Drag something hard across a newly waxed surface and it will look like you have scratched the wood itself. Your explanation that you have "only scratched the wax" will strike most people as whiny and pathetic.

Whatever you choose, be consistent. When it comes time to "renew" that Stickley morris chair, use wax or oil and never alternate. Putting oil over wax accomplishes nothing. However penetrating the oil may be, it will be blocked from contact with the wood by the sealer of wax. Wax over oil is just as bad. The oil itself will catch a mess of dust which will be sealed to the surface by the overcoat of wax.

And use neither product on newly minted furniture. Some of it's made as described above. All the rest, however pricey, is day-old corn slurry over a base of Cheese Curls. It is then waved before a vat of Formica and finished off with a melt of jujubes. Using a good paste wax on any of this trash would be as odd as Chanel No. 5 on a pit bull. Just hose it down and call it a day.

All of which brings us back to dusting. Once you've cleaned and finish-coated your furniture, you can attend to the little particles of flotsam that continue to blow in from Kitty and Michael. The best thing here is an impregnated dust cloth. For masculinity freaks, that will sound appealing, though pro-choice activists may be put off by the sound.

fig. 38. Top-quality dust cloths arrive at a military encampment. At no point in his career should a man neglect dusting.

An impregnated cloth is simply a treated rag with enough threshold tackiness to be a lure to dust. That means that when you wipe a dirty surface, dust will cling to the cloth instead of recolonizing elsewhere. My mother loves these and I love her. Or rather she loaned me exactly enough money to buy a sandwich on two installments. Low-interest loans create the warmest bonds and I recommend impregnated rags as a tribute to her.

The other alternative is Lemon Pledge or any product that professes to work similarly. Looking back, I was probably harsh. Lemon Pledge may be all that it says. For all I know it cleans and polishes and dusts and waxes and does plate tectonics. I once attended a course on "Sylvia Plath and Removing Stains from Porcelain Oven Doors," taught by an immensely articulate can of Pledge.

What I do know is that it works on a dust cloth. That means it'll generate sufficient tackiness so that the dust you swipe will end up on the rag. More than that, I cannot tell. When every adman is sent to Leavenworth, I'll be riding into a redeemed Jerusalem.

As for alternative technologies of swiping dust, I hereby pronounce a solemn anathema. Feather dusters of any sort are the Oscar Wilde of international housecleaning. Pick one up in your dandified hand and you'll be branded immediately as a masculinity outlaw. I wouldn't touch one if it were made of gold, although I might be tempted to take a look if it came attached to a high-performance growth fund.

fig. 39. A feather duster may be fine for tickling the rumps of insignificant dogs, but they are unfit for use by a male housecleaner.

Sheep's-wool dusters are not a particle better, although they don't convey quite the same note of semiotic ambiguity. My experience is that they simply fail; without a *real* hand holding a *real* dusting cloth, the dust never seems to get gathered up.

Besides, they look like lambs on a stick. There's nothing I know that's more repulsive except, perhaps, a state-fair corn dog.

CHAPTER ELEVEN

BDELLIUM IS THERE, AND LAPIS LAZULI

Back off, buddy, *I* write the titles. You want titles, write a book. In the meantime, I'll stick with stubbornness. I hate being edited. I hate having to *talk* to people. Why should I let some feedbag functionary mess around with my deathless prose?

Anyone I care about will recognize the reference: the description from Genesis of the land of Havilah. It's a list of things that won't wilt in combat, *like the surfaces that typify the late-twentieth-century home.* I knew you would get it if I simply went more slowly. Some people need custodial care and others manage with just occasional help.

The basic idea is that we are surrounded by substances which stand and deliver before the roughest customers. A goose-down comforter may be great for bedtime, but would you want to use it as a kitchen countertop? It would be absurd, unthinkable, contrary to nature, like three Republican administrations in a row.

Our ancestors, of course, knew from tiles. There's a notable mosaic from the ruins of Pompeii that uses crumbs and fish bones as part of its design. The idea was that you would fall down drunk after dinner and be suffused with amusement at the cleverness of the mosaicist. "Mine gods, that looks like a real olive pit. Did I do that, or is it part of the design? Ha, ha, ha; Proconsul, look here!" Me, I think it's a one-joke floor. Give me something really funny, like parquet tiles backed with adhesive.

The problem is that things have gotten vastly more complicated. Let's just say that you're a yuppie slimeball, married in the seventies with a banana-spice wedding cake. Maybe there were candied violets on the buttercream and a scattering of edible nasturtiums on the arugula.

None of this really concerns me at all except as an indication of your lockstep conformism. Sometime soon in the middle of the night, ask yourself why you bother at all. Face it, guy, you're a fashion lemming, rushing toward the chasm of blended oneness. You're a newt, a school-fish, an extra in *Triumph of the Will*; you're a failure in the game of healthy individuation.

What really interests me is that, simple as that, there's a Michael Graves teakettle sitting on your stove top. Don't play dumb: You know what I mean. It's the truncated cone with the periwinkle handle. And stuffed into the spout is a stupid little plug shaped like a bird in some odd wine color.

fig. 40. "Look, Dear! That mosaic cat seems almost startlingly lifelike!"

That's if you never used the kettle. If you use it regularly you dumped the bird; what the hell were you supposed to do with it? Stuff it in the spout between occasional boilings? Did Michael Graves actually imagine that we would keep it on hand so that we could stuff it *continually*?

My real question, though, is altogether different. This isn't a book on washing dishes, but Michael's kettle is a window on the world. I know that the body of the kettle is stainless steel. But the handle and the bird and the little knob on the kettle top are made of something I've never seen before. All I can say is that it feels hard and solid, and it stays moderately cool when the kettle is boiling.

But I have no real sense of what it is and *no real sense of how to clean it.* And that goes double if you've plopped it down on the newfangled stove top your brother-in-law sold you. That's the kind where a glassy hot spot begins to glow when you hit the dial. What exactly could that H-spot be? And what happens if it gets doused with a marinara?

And that, my friends, is the story of our lives. Being nominally present in the twentieth century means being surrounded by a profusion of durable surfaces quite different from those experienced by our ancestors. They had a few simple things like logs and dirt. We've got anodized aluminum and high-impact plastic. We've got Lexan, Corian, latex, and melamine. And on top of that, the plastic laminates, all in perennial disrepair. "Look, Proconsul, it's a strip of Formica, partly detached from its plywood base material."

How to cope with the mess in the kitchen? Put a gun to my head and I couldn't say. The shelves in the grocery store tell a story of particularity. One man, one vote, one surface, one cleanser. Buy this for that and *nothing* else. It's as tightly focused as *tae kwon do*.

fig. 41. A Michael Graves teakettle is one of housekeeping's great challenges. But don't allow yourself to be dwarfed by the task.

Got a kryptonite cupboard with polyvinyl handles? By God, boy, you're in luck today. We just got a shipment from Alpha Centauri. It's a great-little-product-smells-just-like-lemons. Just remember to wear Kevlar overalls; that stuff'll take the tread off a tire. But it beats the pants off anything at Safeway. Takes care of stains like napalm on thatch.

It didn't always used to be that way. A long way back, when dads were dads, moms were free to appear in amateur theatricals. They shopped for bridge mix, watched "I Love Lucy," and enjoyed the advantage of giveaway mortgages. And every so often, when the spirit moved them, they poured an ounce of Jubilee and cleaned every inanimate known to woman.

My very own mother was one of the elect. She was a goddess, a housecleaning divinity, and Jubilee was her cleansing unguent. She used it on everything: porcelain and stainless. She used it on wood and linoleum and Formica. She used it on me. She used it on the dog. That's the trouble with Mom: permeable borders. She never seemed to know where "inanimate" stopped. I asked my therapist if that was bad. She allowed as how it might be *really* bad.

The difference between us is that she felt secure: Jubilee was like money in the bank. It was thick and viscous, like a deflated milkshake. It buffed up beautifully into a sober little shine. It was good and reliable and right with God, the promise of redemption in a sixteen-ounce bottle. It was Jubilee for a hurting world. The very sound of it was the certainty of faith.

So where is Jubilee when you need it? I haven't seen it in a million years. CNN saw a bottle in Bozeman, carefully hoarded by a small-town grocer. There's a persistent rumor that one batch a year is made in the basement of the Keebler cookie tree. It's right after they finish the November Sandies. A few of the guys do it Thanksgiving morning.

But even if you found it, you wouldn't want it. To begin with, nobody *wants* to pour anything. Cleaning in the nineties means spraying from a bottle. Loading Jubilee in the belly of a spray bottle would be about as effective as sucking honey through a straw. You could probably do it, but it would be odd and awful. People would laugh. Your parents would be ashamed.

fig. 42. A European alternative to Jubilee. Especially effective for ethnic cleansing.

The other problem is the simplifications of memory. Do I really know that Jubilee worked, or that it worked on everything in our little house? Maybe it did, maybe it didn't. I tried to ask Mom, but she's not talking. The problem is not a failure of recall; she's alive and lucid, alarmingly so. It seems that I need to call more often and that *she* should be writing this book, not me. It's a little problem we keep running into, like the time she beat me out for shortstop. I tried to tell her that I needed the experience, but she's got this idea about the "American meritocracy."

fig. 43. Man kissed by his wife after having sponge-mopped the ceiling. A pad strapped to the head may be very effective.

Finally, remember that if it cleaned in the fifties, it doesn't mean that it will clean in the nineties. Jubilee might have been great for stainless, but who knows what it would do with melamine. Life and housecleaning are like a moving stream. Everything changes, flowing onward. Water moves from here to there. Little droplets form and reform. Giant bugs crawl across the surface. Catfish suck in great, gasping heaves. Everything everywhere is sickening and polluted. Very soon we're all going to die.

That doesn't mean that there aren't good substitutes. I once bought a bottle of Simple Green which looked like God's own answer to cleaning everything. It was plainly packaged, looked convincingly all-purpose and, saints be praised, it was completely biodegradable.

The trouble is that you needed a chemist to mix it. There were separate dilutions for different uses printed in six-point type on a two-inch label. It meant that in order to use the stuff safely, you had to measure it with an electron microscope. Not that you'd know from the way they sold it: It came on like a sweetheart, in a conventional spray bottle, broadcasting convenience like June Allyson for Depends.

All of which made me feel resentful and mean. I do not want to be humiliated by a cleanser.

CHAPTER TWELVE

WIPE OUT

So there you are in the afterglow of breakfast, arm hairs glued to the syrup run on the table.

My best advice is the middle course. My best advice is *always* the middle course. That's why people buy these books. Radical anything is simply un-American. If you can't imagine it at the Gun and Knife Show, it probably doesn't belong on this continent.

What I advise is to keep your head. Most drips and spills will come up with water and you'll never need to rinse a residue. Get a regular sponge made of supermarket cellulose, take it to the sink, douse and wring. There will be enough to wipe the compromised surface without slopping water on either you or it.

Emphasis here on supermarket cellulose. Those natural sponges for high-end bath takers are a nice little touch for toilet voluptuaries, but they take too much water for household cleaning. If you can't abide a synthetic product, try the pelts of baby seals.

If the job is tougher, you might bring reinforcements: those sponges wrapped in a plastic network. I hate these sponges for regular use. They look for all the world like the real thing. Most people even *call* them sponges. I myself call them a scam: quick-change artists and Machiavellian tricksters. Wipe down a table with a net-wrapped sponge and it will come and go without picking up anything. You might just loosen a melted toffee chip, but the sponge itself has no absorbency. You'll have to come back with a cotton rag or, for the environmentally-impaired, paper towels.

fig. 44. Cellulose kitchen sponges are typically useless during thoracic surgery. However, they do have their champions.

What you've really got is a little plastic scraper, gentle enough for other plastic. The sponge is there to caddy your water and boost the loosening power of the netting. But don't expect a one-shot deal. The sponge will just move water around. Think of it as an old zero-coupon bond. It will bring you close to where you want to be, but never spike you into real security.

When water won't cut it, you'll need to move on. A little while back, I did a hatchet job on mixing, but I have to admit the old-time charm of hauling around a bucket of stuff. It's the real thing: *very* small-town. Every Saturday for twenty-six years, my very own grandfather tore apart his Buick. He scrubbed it with a Q-tip, licked it clean, and put it back together six hours later. All on the lawn in front of the house.

fig. 45. Animal pelts may make the very best wiping cloths. Of course, you have to kill animals to get them. Do not be put off by their anthropomorphic qualities.

At the time I saw it as a real-man thing. If you were a guy, you spent your Saturdays pondering the mysteries of half-stripped lug nuts. Now I recognize him for what he was: a psycho-fetishist with a thing about drive shafts.

It's exactly the same with cleaning solutions: Once again, you could do it all yourself. Plain ammonia will get the job done and the right solution strengths are on the back of the bottle. But what you really need is something in a shpritzer that will work on most things you are likely to clean. There are a hundred available products on the market and the only reason I use Formula 409 is that it's heavily advertised and I'm a sucker for coupons. Also, there's my enduring hope that any product I mention by name will land me a lucrative endorsement contract with a megabucks company into hazardous chemicals. I said it all in the chapters about windows, but in the world of endorsement deals, enough is never enough.

Speaking of windows, a spray for glass will frequently work on other surfaces. I learned that trick from the kindly people who duped us into buying the house we live in. They had a bottle of Windex under the sink and used it for absolutely everything. They especially liked it on sole almondine.

The reverse, however, is not usually true: Other stuff won't work on windows. I have no idea why this should be so, but if you can't trust me, who can you trust?

fig. 46. If you are forced to mix cleaning solutions, it helps to have attractive company. A comfortable diaper and fur galoshes may also make the job go faster.

The thing to do is pay close attention. There'll be plenty of product info on the back, although you might have to read it through two inches of liquid. Funny thing about those megabucks chemical firms. There's always plenty for mergers and acquisitions, but never enough for labels for humans.

In any case, read as you go, even if you need scuba gear to do it. You want the solution to cut through basic mess. We're talking about garden-variety marmalade on wallpaper. Maybe phone cord abrasion on woodwork in your kitchen. You also want something without too many advisories. If it says that it works on practically everything, except plastic, metal, painted surfaces, and wood, it's time to crater the display in the supermarket and make immediate contact with a federal regulatory agency.

Neither should it say too much about testing. If you need to use it first on an inconspicuous place, and then wait for quarterly reports on damage, blow it off and try something else. Testing is why we have *Consumer Reports*. We cannot all expect to be gods.

And beware, again, of the need to rinse. The best people I know get in and get out. They don't ambulate aimlessly or do the same thing twice. If you have to clean with one thing and then rinse with water, you might just as well use dirt as an abrasive and use something else to clean away the dirt. In other words, you've made a really bad choice and there's no alternative except publicly to shame you.

I should mention that all of this falls on deaf ears, at least where Mother Williams is concerned. She's a fiend for rinsing and won't do otherwise. She sees a soap film as the specter of death. I figure that things could be a lot worse. If she spends her time rinsing major appliances, she might not notice that I've moved to Oregon.

There are, of course, more impervious substances that will not rise up to meet your cleaning solution. Here's where things get a little more serious. Up until now, it's been water and sponges, with a transitional movement of cleaning solution and paper towels. The really big shew is dirt so gone that you need an abrasive to bring the job home. The dog vomits on the floor of the laundry room and you find the results six months later. Little Wayne gets a second urge for organ meat and offs a squirrel in an upstairs bathroom. I've got another scenario involving Phyllis Schlafly and a particularly interesting outtake from from *The Silence of the Lambs,* but it would conflict with my commitments to family values.

Now's the time to run for cleanser. That means little granules of housecleaning muscle that will take you down through any accumulation. The problem here is that cleansers are for keeps. The stuff that comes in those little cylinders may look as harmless as grated Parmesan, but what's packed inside works just like sandpaper with the same potential for permanent scratching.

fig. 47. Reading information on the back of the front label may require extraordinary exertions, especially if there is still liquid in the container. Why do manufacturers expect heroics when a simple back label would solve the problem?

The thing to do is to wet the surface you're about to clean, even if it means reactivating the mess. Wet it liberally and your sponge as well. Everything you know may argue against it; moistened vomit seems to come to life, like a desert blooming in a sudden shower. But it's either that or risking scratches; me, I'd opt for Eau de Vomit.

The other thing is to watch yourself carefully. A guy like you could scrape the hell out of practically anything in no time flat. And that's assuming you are properly lubricated. Whatever happens, no granules on Formica. Whatever happens, no granules on Plexiglas. And while I'm at it, no Plexiglas at all. Never, ever, have adult Americans made a fad of anything so utterly stupid. Plexiglas is *wrong*. Plexiglas is *poofta*. You may not suffer for defrauding orphans, but you'll go to hell for choosing Plexiglas.

The final tier of hard-surface madness is the stuff that settles in the throat of the toilet. Every so often you'll look down absently and find the unhappy residue of Christmas past. Don't be frightened; bad things happen. The fact that you live in fetid squalor is not a measure of moral failure. It simply points to the display of incontinence you venture courageously to call a life.

The shelves are full of products to help you and, once again, it's a festival of specificity. There's a special category for the bowl of the toilet and something else to clean the sink. There are scrubbers intended for soap film on porcelain and others still to handle grout. This is serious dirt, and American business has offered its hand in housecleaning partnership.

All I can say is cut the crap. And cut it with a dilute solution of bleach. That's chlorine bleach—Clorox is perfect. And it's safe when mixed with nothing except water. That's right, nitpickers, I said mix. Just this once and never again. Say no to pricey convenience products, pumped with packaging and unnecessary additives. Say no to toxins flushed at home, then on and out into the American landscape.

Chlorine bleach will do it all and just as quickly as anything else. You'll need gloves for you, a sponge and a brush, and a pail to hold the solution of bleach. It'll all be over in no time flat and may never need to be done again.

"Never" here is a technical term that actually means three months later. Here's a thought: On the day you do your quarterly estimates, give your toilet a hit of bleach. The IRS will never know of the hostile irony in your domestic schedule.

Beyond all this, there's nothing to say, at least for middle-class guys like you. Rich people simply have more to worry about. Brass is separate and so is marble. The same with the grate on your outdoor grill: swordfish steaks and mahi-mahi are hell and a half to delaminate properly. This is a book for middle-class people who want nothing more from life than an Egg

McMuffin. You corporate types are on your own. If you're so great, just figure it out.

fig. 48. A devoted husband presents his wife with a special device to clean her barbecue pit. Such items call for careful handling.

On the other hand, you could fly me in for my special seminar on "Housecleaning Hints for the Corporate Man." It's the best buy around in leadership development and I'm currently accepting requests for appearances. It's the real thing: overheads and videos and break-out groups for problematic scenarios. Malcolm Forbes used to love it. See him in my video on "Gemstone Toilet Handles."

CHAPTER THIRTEEN

SCAM CLEANING
FOR COMPANY

Many otherwise sensible people believe that they will be forced to entertain their bosses at home. I used to be confused about the source of all of this, until I revisited the fourth episode of "Bewitched." Then and there I suddenly realized that it had determined the foundations of life as we know it.

A few minutes after the second commercial break, Darin the First impulsively asks Larry to leave a little early and come over for "cocktails." At a moment in history when fun has ceased, it may be hard to remember that white persons once gathered in the late afternoon to smear Cheez Whiz on Ritz crackers and do truckloads of alcohol. Larry, himself, responds with eagerness. Despite his loathing for the oleaginous Darin, he is the great problem drinker of sixties television. A heartbeat later he is swilling big-time.

From that point forward the die is cast. Larry is always dropping by for refreshments, hoping that Samantha will do something flambé. Darin grows increasingly twitchy, hysterical that his wife's truly massive gifts will dwarf his skills as a jingle writer for cookie products. I vaguely remember an eyebrow thing that registers each flush of paranoid imagining; looking at the screen becomes physically painful. And Elizabeth Montgomery expends her television life *preparing for the moment of Larry's arrival!* Only the honed contempt of Agnes Moorehead makes any of this guano marginally tolerable. Ask a hundred humans, male or female, who've achieved modest success in a lifetime of labor, and they'll tell you they owe it all to Endora.

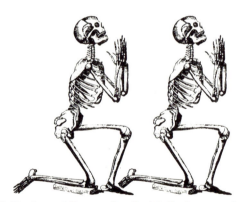

fig. 49. Darin and Larry plead with Endora to change them back.

My point is that all of this was a lie. The simple fact is that if your boss is normal, he will probably never come to your house and you will never have to clean it beforehand. First of all, who's got a boss? Right up to AIDS, we did serial monogamy. Now that that's over, we're doing serial employment. The last time I saw a boss of mine, they had locked his keyboard and laid out the packing boxes. I just love it when they make the big boys cry.

As for the remaining few, it pays to remember that the corporate code says suck *up*, not down. Why would a boss waste time at your house, when he could be wriggling his pumpkin in *his* boss's deck chair. The key achievement for American men is to be invited over for alpha male hot dogs. It may not be tactful to say so publicly, but you probably aren't coded for quick calling on *anyone's* car phone.

None of this, however, means that you're safe. As long as there are mothers, *none* of us is safe. At this very moment, regardless of the hour, your own mother is planning to come to see you. She may protest that she was the one who bore you, who nursed you through earaches and your first divorce. She may even be right about the magnitude of her sacrifice. But that only makes her more determined to get even, and she will stop at nothing to take you out, even to the point of *visiting your house.*

If that happens, nothing can save you. She will walk through the door trailing vapors of disapproval and turn your life into self-esteem hash. She may even be bearing *this very book* in an effort to raise your consciousness about housecleaning.

"This E. Todd is such a nice boy. Why can't you be smart and successful like he is? I bet he bought his mother a condo with the royalties."

Remember one thing: I'm on your side, at least until I see her proof of purchase. I'm here for *you*, guy, not some shrieking crone pretending to be your biological parent. Follow my advice and you'll make it through. It won't be pretty, but it beats the alternative. If you hurt your mother, the state will kill you and nobody employs the lethally injected.

One

First things first, *discard the take-out cartons.* I know this seems like a trivial matter, beneath the dignity of a high-end guide. But twenty-seven cartons variously stuffed with the remains of your private obsession with cold Szechuan noodles do not register with most people as gracious living. Notice that when you open a magazine, the homes of the stars are furnished with chairs, and not waist-high mounds of cardboard from The Forbidden Dumpling. This is a subtle point for a certain segment of society, but then so is nose picking on national television. Things that would be fine at a papal investiture are simply not done when you're chatting it up with Arsenio.

fig. 50. Take-out cartons have their legitimate uses. You may use your smallest ones for starting indoor fires.

The problem, of course, is their sheer profusion. The individual box may seem unassuming, but taken collectively, they are sexual adventurers. Any two boxes taken from the restaurant will produce four other boxes by the time you get home. And I am speaking about cartons of either sex. The one last night from my *moo goo gai pan* played the part of Stanley in *A Streetcar Named Desire*.

These little babes are also weirdly indestructible. A sanitary landfill in Pismo Beach, California, was recently excavated by urban archaeologists. To no one's surprise, it was *shtupped* with take-out cartons, some dating back to the seventeenth century. I wouldn't have believed it, but I saw it myself.

My best advice is to use yourself as a compactor. Stand a foot away from the kitchen counter. Insert a dead box between yourself and the Formica and push forward to crumple the box in half. It wouldn't be complete without a grunt. It's the only way to put an end to their promiscuity. Look around after you're done. You'll see many things≈tables, sofas, your spouse—that may not have been visible since the last elections.

Two

My second suggestion is to *send your children to boarding school*. If company's coming there may be no alternative. The same is true if company is your mother. It may be tempting to assume that she wants to see her grandchildren, but never forget the real reason for her visit. She's coming for the sole purpose of declaring you a pig and wishing volubly that she had chosen therapeutic abortion.

As for kids and housecleaning, I stand my ground: Kids are to dirt what Bush is to stomach flu. There's something about them beyond simple magnetism. Monzo, my six-year-old, is the classic case. Insects worship at the throne of his chair, knowing that enough will fall from his fork to feed their descendants from now till Orkin-time. No straight line can stand in his presence; he can rearrange plaids through telekinesis. It's like the scene in *Carrie* where thoughts become knives, except, in our case, thoughts become underwear, tinged with earth tones and wedged behind the toilet bowl. It's an amazing ability, but profoundly antisocial. Lucky for us, West Point accepts six-year-olds.

I say pack 'em off and be done with it. Your children may whimper, but that's life in Hooverville. Eventually they'll see the rightness of it all. In the scheme of the Creator, the claims of family take their place behind a sparkling toaster oven. Which is better: a well-adjusted child or a bathroom sink without a lurking snot ball? Don't ask me; go ask your mother. She's the one with the blister pack of contraceptives.

fig. 51. Not every child is the enemy of orderliness. A very large child may be trusted to do a certain amount of housecleaning. A gigantic child may be useful in maintaining public buildings.

Three

My final advice is a piece of desperation. When all else fails, *create a distraction*. Real estate agents know all about this. Just last week, I walked into hell, packaged as a three-bedroom English cottage trade-up. Everything leaked, beginning with the cats. The floor in the basement had gone geologic. There is something unsettling about seeing a clothes dryer teeteringly perched on a Mesozoic uplift.

But in the kitchen, where the heart is, a little cauldron of mulling spices was working its magic. Instead of cat scat there was cinnamon and ginger, and promises of fresh bread and children and military school. You, too, can be a real estate agent every time someone walks through the door.

Worried that Mom will see fly-specks on the microwave? As soon as she arrives tell her that you're married and ask her why she wasn't at the wedding, particularly since your wife is a Wrigley heiress. Picking a fight is a sure-fire gambit and will likely result in more intermittent visits.

Alternatively you could create a physical disturbance. Invite a swimming pool company to begin excavation and cancel the contract before the cement is poured. Make sure to specify the front of the house. This is especially good for persistent visitors. People will begin to think of you as Boo Radley, a harmless recluse, but all-around good guy.

Finally, you could simply feign madness or die. In the presence of depression, everyone thinks Prozac, but they'll still wonder why you can't get the hair out of the bathtub. Madness is better because it's so pitiable and dear. Look what it's done for Ronald Reagan. Nobody would think of asking those nasty little questions about bargaining with Khomeini the day before the election.

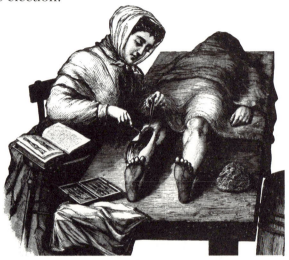

fig. 52. While feigning death may be off-putting to others, your mother may decide to look further into the matter.

But in the last analysis dead may be best. In the presence of dead people, most people leave. They don't really care about dishes in the sink. And they certainly won't care about a little dust on the baseboards. Nine out of ten will run out of the house shrieking. And isn't that what you really wanted in the first place?

CHAPTER FOURTEEN

DANGER, WILL ROBINSON, DANGER!

Nothing about housecleaning is really dangerous. The most that could happen is that you'll blow a circuit breaker, or maybe suck a gerbil into the belly of the vacuum cleaner.

In my own experience that happened just once, in Huntsville, Alabama, in 1967. But the ultimate results were disastrous to all. Billy Axeflesh, distraught and hurting, rigged a shotgun to the automatic garage door opener to off his offending father for keeps. It was supposed to discharge when Dad hit the remote, blasting the door and Axeflesh to the plot at Calvary.

Unfortunately, it got little Billy himself when Dad pulled into the driveway about five minutes early. Crossing the pavement for a better view, Billy got bookended between the gun and the button, and Mr. Axeflesh got splattered with little pieces of Billy. Everybody managed to get to dinner that night, but things were never the same at the homestead again.

Nothing remotely like this will happen to you. *Au contraire*: just the opposite. Thrushes will sing and the gods will smile at the sight of a man wiping down baseboards. I've known men just like you who opened their front doors to find powder-blue Jaguars sitting in their driveways, delivered by womenfolk appreciative of their efforts.

Work at it long enough and claim the keys to heaven. While the rest of us slave in the Third Chasm of Hell, choking on last year's blackened red fish, you'll be feasting on Leviathan in the throne room of God. Voltaire was right: The *jardin* is here, second door to the right beyond the phone jack.

At the same time, I feel compelled to remind you that being stupid comes naturally to most of us, and what happened in Huntsville could happen to you. Not the part about the hamster or Billy's earlobe; Alabama and the baroque are close personal friends. Other states do gore with a certain dignified restraint.

I worry most about things like variations on bleach. Like bleach and ammonia. Bleach and toilet bowl cleaner. Bleach and orange juice or tonic water or V-8. For those of you who were hand-gouging nut dishes in wood shop while the girls down the hall learned the really useful things in home ec., bleach and anything is a lethal combination. It may be helpful to think of bleach as a Kalashnikov. Don't do anything fancy and you will keep your body parts.

fig. 53. A housecleaning man will be judged highly desirable. A certain kind of woman may find you hugely attractive.

And what exactly happens if you err? What happens when bleach and ammonia are combined? I tried it once just to see what would happen. Immediately the bathroom was filled with smoke and Ibsen's Troll King appeared on the toilet seat. An unholy choir chanted "Trond of the Valfjeld" while the Troll King himself devoured the dog. Actually, that would have been bad enough, but he fastidiously insisted on starting with the eyes.

Do not step into this world of terror. At least not without a very large dog.

fig. 54. A mixture of bleach and ammonia *could* have inconsistent effects. Combinations of the two may shrink adults and make children dance.

CHAPTER FIFTEEN

FUN AND GAMES WITH VENETIAN BLINDS

I know I should be making all of this sound easy, but a real guidebook has a different purpose. It may look accessible, even empowering, but its central aim is pathological dependence.

I casually mention a few small matters, making you think that you're going to accomplish something. And then I bury you alive with facts and babble, a slush of technical terms and strategies. The result, please God, is that you think you need me; that the basic choice is me or institutionalization.

I wish, of course, that all of this were true. Nothing at all would please me more than abject loyalty and a nice fat royalty check. But you and I know another truth: Success in housecleaning is beyond the best of us. The men I know were built for caves, not waxing baseboards in the upstairs powder room. The real answer is to put scruples aside and *persuade a houseguest to do it for you.*

We are used to thinking in other terms. My wife imagines that our guests are treasures, existing only to be coddled and pampered. She buys special foods, like bread and milk, whenever a long-lost friend comes by. Our children seem to enjoy it, too. They get to sit on real chairs and leave the basement at least once a day.

fig. 55. The proper relationship between guidebook and user. The figure on the left is the personification of the guidebook.

I see it all in another way: The average houseguest is a ready resource for tasks that would make a grown man weep. I think immediately of venetian blinds, a well-known cause of Balkan fratricide. I recently had a vision of Hell in which they were prominently featured in an inner circle, smack in the middle of the recently disemboweled. Lee Atwater was there with one of those gloves where each of the fingers is a spongy cylinder, made for dragging between the slats. Couldn't get it on for love or money.

fig. 56. A happy guest removes dead animals for his grateful host. It is easy to turn your friends into cooperative drudges.

How to get a houseguest to help? You won't even have to *think* of asking. The average houseguest, male or female, is pathetically fearful of becoming a burden. Here, again, my wife helped to educate me. Her unbreakable rule when staying as a guest is never, ever use other people's towels.

I have tried to say that we *need* to use them; that our hosts might even *want* us to use them as an alternative, say, to soaking their upholstery. She remains adamant and dries herself with Kleenex. It takes an hour and a half and two boxes of Kleenex, but better anything than actually using their towels.

Think on this when you're entertaining guests. A social visit is the very best time to turn your friends into slaves and automatons. Just quietly leave a pail on the landing and your guests will respond to the subliminal suggestion. Just like that they'll be washing curtains, stripping floors, and cleaning storm windows.

And don't forget the mildewed tile grout. They could even use their very own toothbrushes.

CHAPTER SIXTEEN

A LITTLE WHINING

By now I bet I know what you're thinking.

"Gee, E. Todd, you're the greatest! This is even better than your first book, the justly famed *First Men's Guide to Ironing*. How much funnier can one guy get? It's like 'Hints from Heloise meets Bertolt Brecht!'

"But where's the part about cleaning window screens? And what about that machine they advertise on television, with the big green woman in the skin-tight exercise pants? Can you really steam your carpets at home? And what about spraying Windex on my computer screen? Are all glass cleaners useable with Windows?"

Don't get me wrong; I know the answers. Whisk brooms. Bogus. No. Damp rag. No. The problem is a thing called market-driven publishing: Since there is no market, there is no publishing. On April 12, 1954, a woman in Idaho read a postcard from her cousin Becky. That was the last time anyone read in America.

The result of all of this is books like these: quickie treatments of complex issues. Ruthless cutting. Forced-march prose. My contract called for 124 pages, lots of pictures, and little paragraphs. Don't whine at me, you little dust ball. I did the best I could in the space available.

Now where's the address for the lady in Idaho? For the record, my name is Becky.